AF198049

Interaktionen
Interactivities

by/von

Motschi von Richthofen

Gedichte/Poems
English/German

tredition GmbH
1. Auflage 2017
Copyright 2017 by
Motschi von Richthofen und
tredition GmbH

tredition GmbH
Sitz der Gesellschaft: Hamburg
E-Mail: info@tredition.de
Geschäftsführung: Sönke Schulz, Sandra Latußeck

ISBN
978-3-7439-3154-1 (Paperback)
978-3-7439-3155-8 (Hardcover)
978-3-7439-3156-5 (e-Book)

Achte auf Deine Gedanken,
denn sie werden Worte.
Achte auf Deine Worte,
denn sie werden Handlungen.
Achte auf Deine Handlungen,
denn sie werden Gewohnheiten.
Achte auf Deine Gewohnheiten,
denn sie werden Dein Charakter.
Achte auf Deinen Charakter,
denn er wird Dein Schicksal.

Talmud mündliche Lehre der Gesetze und religiösen Überlieferungen des Judentums nach der Babylonischen Gefangenschaft

Dreamers

Dreamers always changed the human trace
They got an idea of an incredible place
And believe in it and transform this imagination
Into a real and realizable mission.

People like to sneer at those idealists
Cause they are not conform to all formalists

Dreamers always sow a seed of the unbelievable
Looking beyond what's achievable

Lovers impatience

I fell in love to you at the first sight
You were lightly dressed and bright

But than came the impatience along
And instead of being strong

I let myself go much to fast
And was not me any more
Insane but it is now the past
And I closed the lovers door

Eagerness is sometimes great
In the right moment the best way
Which opens a new gateway

In love it is often the other way around
Mid aged humans with one love in their life
They are cautious where their soul may dive

Fracking

The process of trilling down in the ground
Oil and money deeply confound
And nowhere a turn around.

Using a huge amount of precious liquidness
What kind of insane business
And fiscal-energized success.

We are intelligent creature in this universe
We have got eyes and observe
To greedy others most diverse.

Renewable energy should be given priority
Like the sun or wind a bulk commodity
These will be our economical entity.

We see a turn around
Most profound

A new Process
And progress

The human nurse
With a far-sighed purse

A long-term facility
Becoming a reality

Refugee

I left my home, my roots
Wearing just one pair of boots
My whole family was killed
And our life imperiled
I am a normal pacifist
Don't want to rise my fist
I believe in a sort of lord
Who never would take a sword
to destroy others in his name
What a destructive game

I left my home, my friends
With nothing in my hands
I tried to escape this insanity
to find a place of humanity
Germany might be this place
with generosity and grace.
A country of fortune and peace
Where my strength may increase
And peace will be a part
with this new start.

I left my home, my family and friends
I left my homeland and my roots

Nowadays Inquisition

For Gods sake Archimedes writings
were discovered in our century,
If not in the Christian killings,
greater would have been the injury.

For the Middle Ages and their citizens,
this cup passed thanks heavens.

They even founded
the Congregation of the Holy Office.
Many were wounded,
because of narrow mind disservice.

They even executed
people with different visions.
And as well persecuted
Humans with open perceptions.

Secularization was the best to establish
and Christian inquisition to abolish.

Today we got another religion,
which does the same.
They have a destructive mission
in Allah's name.

For peaceful people of our time
It is just an insane crime.

Islamic State based on intolerance

makes no sense.
All democratic States got tolerance
a peace defense.

600 years back in their evolution
what a terrifying-pitiful revolution.

Secularization is the best to establish
and Islamic inquisition to abolish.

From inside the only way
They have to find the right trace
We all just humbly pray
For all of them and a better place.

Inquisition der Neuzeit

Machtkampf basierend auf Religion
Ein alt bekanntest Mittel
Zerstörung als wichtige Mission
Umhüllt vom Glaubenskittel

Alles im Namen von der fiktiven Gestalt
Ob Gott, Allah oder Jehova
Unrealistisch, da durchdrungen von Gewalt
Für einige noch nicht so klar

Am Ende geht es nur um Macht
Und wenn Staat und Religion noch unter einem Dach
Dann ist es eine leichte Schlacht
Denn die Gläubigen sind die Bauern in diesem Schach.

Jetzt sind wir schon im 21igstern Jahrhundert
Und was mich verwundert
Ist diese unglaubliche Scheuklappenhaltung
Was für eine Veranstaltung

Heine hat es schon gesagt "Wenn ich an Deutschland denke in der Nacht
So bin ich um den Schlaf gebracht"
So sage ich, „Wenn ich an Deutschland denke in der momentanen Situation
So hoffe ich auf rechtsstaatliche Integration"

Wirklich

Ich hatte viel gesehen
Konnte vieles auch verstehen
Und doch hat es meine Seele geschlagen
Wie konnte ich das nur alles nur ertragen
Armut verkrampft mein Herzensgewissen
Es wird mir schier just rausgerissen.
Ja klar, ich weiß Menschen haben Freude in sich
Und verändern das Sein für mich und für dich.

Beach

Walking along the beach
eternity I can reach
Every day a new painted beauty
an awesome reality,
designed for the soul to see
with joy and glee.

Walking along the beach
composure I can reach
The waves softly approaching
and mellow speaking
A warm music to the heart
here and there a lizard.

Walking along the beach
strength I can reach
The ocean wild and furious
changing my conscious
strengthening my perceptions
supporting my ambitions

Walking along the beach
million of things to reach
Every moment a pleasure
wonderful und pure

Walking on the beach
to learn and to teach

Windmühlen

Don Quichotte hat oft viel zu kämpfen
um die Gemüter zu dämpfen
jetzt in die weitere Zukunft zu denken
und so Energie zu lenken
kann ja leider nur ein kleiner Teil
ein menschlicher Nachteil.

Der Wind er kommt und elektrifiziert
Strom wird produziert
weitergeleitet über Trassen
und beleuchtet die Gassen

Sobald die Windmühle steht
und der Wind weht
ist die Emission Vergangenheit
und zur Zufriedenheit
für den reinen Fortschritt
im Konsumritt

Flying

Icarus was the first
he had this thirst
for reach the sky
and he had to die

Da Vinci came next
brought it into context
with mechanical invention
an extraordinary intention.

Lilienthal used his own design
stayed in the air for some time
but failed in the end
no more life in his hand

The brother Wright
both bold and bright
and developed a plane
a milestone to proclaim

More and more inventions
with good and bad intentions
and so man could fly
to the endless sky

Der Hund

Ein guter Freund
ein Herz an Seele

Nur Liebe mehr nicht
bedingungslos einfach

Ein ehrlicher Freund
ohne Hintergrundgedanken.

Nur Liebe geben
ohne zu erwarten.

Ein wahrer Freund
immer für einen da

Nur Liebe empfindend
immer verstehend

Korruption

Sobald Korruption auftritt
geht man den ersten Schritt
in Richtung Negativität
und weg von Qualität

Ein Einzelner sucht seinen Vorteil
für die Gemeinschaft zum Nachteil

Sobald jemand bestechlich ist
Haben wir den Mist
Gewissen verliert sich recht schnell
und leider oft reell

Ein Einzelner sucht seinen Vorteil
für die Gemeinschaft zum Nachteil

Ob Südamerika, Afrika oder Russland
oder in Asien so manches Land
es ist eine Krankheit ohne Grenzen
und gefährdet damit Existenzen.

Ein Einzelner sucht seinen Vorteil
für die Gemeinschaft zum Nachteil

Ob der kleine Mann oder der Minister
jeder zieht seine eigenen Register
und bereichert nur seinen engsten Raum
und zerstört den humanitären Traum.

Ein Einzelner sucht seinen Vorteil

für die Gemeinschaft zum Nachteil

Nun man möge es mir verwehren,
aber ich möchte mich hier beschweren

Manche Bande ist manchmal nun mal da
Und ist wichtiger, das ist wohl kla'

Der Stein

So wundervoll
So voller Kraft
Einfach richtig toll
Einfach sagenhaft

Oft uralt
Oft weich
Eine Gestalt
Ein Königreich

Manchmal Negation
Manchmal Obligation
Viel kommunizieren
Viel exzerpieren

Wohl ein Prunkstück
Wohl ein Lebensglück
Diese Sekunde im Rohzustand
Diese nächste Sekunde ein Brillant.

So einzigartig
in der Struktur
So gewaltig
als Geisteskultur

Oft unerkannt
In Flussbett liegend
Oft erkannt
Und siegend.

Damals als Stein
Noch unvollkommen
Dann hat das Sein
Gestalt angenommen.

Ob Kieselstein
Ob Marmorstein
Ob Edelstein
Ob Heilstein

DER STEIN DER WEISEN.

Die Leinwand der Emotionen

Filme fesseln oft alle Sinne
Bilder aneinandergereiht
Innere seelische Zugewinne
Das Spektrum ist breit

Emotionen an die Wand geworfen
Sie werden gesehen und mitempfunden
Vorstellungen werden entworfen
Traumländer erzeugt und erfunden

Einzigartig und lebendig
Oft alles sehr aufwendig
Geradezu Unglaublich
Manchmal unwirklich

Der Zeit entfliehen
Masken anziehen
Ein anderer Raum
Ein Lebenstraum.

My beloved tooth

Again you wanted to kill me
You tried your very best
Fortunately you did not succeed

Again give it a try and you will see
You convulse my chest
Fortunately you did not succeed

What so ever to see behind the time
On the edge of death
Above all those beautiful sensations

Where so ever I started to clime
On the mountain path
Above all those timeless creations

Smooth the tooth
Fantastic when possessing qualification
Terrible when in bad condition

Forsooth the tooth
A master of the digestion
A supporter of destruction

Leistungszwang

Grotesk, und abnormal
Das ist ja ein Jammertal
Und warum verdammt nochmal
Leistung ist doch keine Qual

Spaß daran haben
Erkenne deine Gaben

Bloß keinen Zwang
Ich verspüre einen Drang
Und lausche dem Klang
Dem Aktionsgesang

Begegnungen

Wundervoll und neue Welten
Mit Mensch und Natur
Eine gemeinsame Tour
Wie lange kann keiner sagen

Wundersam und eine Berührung
Zwischen menschlichen Wesen
Ein zartes Seelenlesen
Oft fürs ganze Leben

Wunderbar und eine Bereicherung
Alle Sinne werden geweckt
tausend Bilder erweckt
ganz gleich in welcher Richtung

How do I love you

There are million ways my heart belongs to you
You might change your points of view
And grow older by time
And when I see gray hairs
I will love them in the way I love you

Together we grow and develop ourselves
day by day

There are million ways my soul embraces yours
You might develop distinct peculiarities
And grow wiser by time
And when I see these oddities
I will love them in the way I love you

Together we grow and develop ourselves
day by day

There are million ways my mind is connected to yours
You might be stubborn in regard of an idea
And grow militant by time
And when I see this funny bullishness
I will love them in the way I love you

Together we grow and develop ourselves
day by day

There are million ways my spirit love yours
You might have difficult times
And grow sad or happy

And when I see your different moods
I will love them in the way I love oyu

Together we grow and develop ourselves
day by day

Architektur

Mehr als nur Baukunst
Symbolisiert sie auch Lebenskunst

Das Einfangen des Raum/Zeitkontinuums
Vieler Menschen und des Individuums

Die Transformation von Licht und Schatten
Hier Fliesen dort Schieferplatten

Die reine Kraft der Phantasie
Visuell geformte Harmonie

Dem Raum wird freie Entfaltung eingehaucht
Durch ihn In Strukturen und Formen eingetaucht

Oft stehen wir nur davor und blicken
Mit Erstaunen und Verzücken

Wundervoll und oft eine Komposition
Einer materialisierten Vision

Jede Epoche bringt einzigartiges hervor
Und öffnet der Zukunft ein weiteres Tor

Sprachschatz

Die Sprache ist verloren
Alles nur noch von Fäkalien durchdrungen
Einfaches für die Ohren
Heurika die Scheisse wird heut besungen

Alles ist nur noch cool und geil
In der Hand das schicke Ekelbeil
Nur weiter so mit dem Mother Fucker Gesang
Ist doch ein super verständlicher Farbklang
Den halt jeder easy versteht
Und mit dem Beat mitgeht
Echt klasse zeugt ja von Tiefe
Prima wie ich vor Dreck triefe

Die Vielfalt ist weg
Hey hallo nur nicht zu viel denken
Es hat auch kein Zweck
Hochtrabenden Gedanken in Worte zu schwenken

Die Masse muss es ja mitkommen
Die ist von zu viel Input krass benommen
Ich bin eine Frau des Volkes und spreche
Ich zahle meine eigene Zeche
Halts Maul und hör einfach zu
Guten Abend München hier bist du
Eine Stadt mit Herz und mehr nicht
Geh mit mir nicht zu hart zu Gericht

Meine Fresse und wenn schon
Worte sind ja nur Rauch und Schall

Gebt mir ein Grammofon
ich besinge den aufsteigenden Fall

Die Suffragetten

Die Suffragetten
Die Netten
Haben Briefkästen in die Luft gejagt
Und damaligen Zustände beklagt
Ihnen haben wir es zu verdanken
Dass die uralten Schranken
Teilweise geöffnet wurden
Hier der Tapferkeitsorden.

Manche sind aber dennoch
im Patriarchaten Loch
Man glaubt es kaum
Es Ist auch kein Traum

Maria schwanger und freut sich schon
Gerade neu in ihrer Position
Geht zu ihrem Chef mit nem lockeren Ton
"Ich bekomme bald nen Sohn"
Die Führungskraft ein Mann
Der aus seiner Haut nicht kann
"Da fallen sie uns ja weg"
Und sie ganz keck
"Wir brauchen neue Steuerzahler
Besonders für sie Herr Thaler"
Da blieb ihm glatt die Spucke weg
Ja so ein Dreck
Etwas verwirrt stammelte er dann
"Was haben sie nur getan"
"Wilden Sex und noch viel mehr
das fiel uns gar nicht schwer"

Darauf konn er nichts mehr sagen
Noch nicht mal sich beklagen.

Am Abend dann zu Haus
Erzählte sie alles Klaus
Und der wie immer mit nem Lachen
"Dem hast du es gezeigt dem Drachen
Na ja auf jeden Fall
Ein echter Affenstall
Ist halt noch ne andere Generation
Mit der Frau am Herd die Vision"
"Halt nicht so ganz bei Verstand
Egal bald sind die auch im Ruhestand
Ach du Klaus
Wie siehts denn aus,
Hast du schon Urlaub genommen"
"Ja klar hab ihn auch bekommen
den Wickelkurs hab ich auch besucht
man hab ich geflucht,
gar nicht mal so einfach
und schwieriger als Schach"

Georg Sand hat als erstes damit angefangen
und ist in Männerhosen rumgegangen
Hypatia noch viel früher schon
an der Uni mit nem neugierigen Ton.

Der Pizzabäcker

Zuerst wird der Ofen angeheizt
bis er die richtigen Grade hat
Nicht unter- oder überheizt
für die Pizza einfach adäquat

Gleich wird der Belag vorbereitet
mit leckeren und guten Zutaten
und viele verschiedene Aromaten
und der feine Teig zubereitet

Jetzt kommt der beste Part
Der Teig wird in der Luft jongliert
Der Pizzakünstler geht an den Start
und ist leidenschaftlich motiviert

Der dünne Teigteller wird hingelegt
mit Tomatensoße fein gestrichen
Hier und da auch ausgeglichen
und dann mit Freuden bunt belegt

Die Komposition der Leidenschaft
wird auf den Schieber gegeben
und behutsam und ohne Kraft
in den Ofen hineingegeben.

Hin und her gedreht und geschoben
damit die Hitze überall hinstrahlt
und ein rundes Gourmetbild malt
geradezu legendenumwoben.

Zu guter Letzt wird sie herausgeholt
und auf den Teller gebracht
und das Ganze unendlich oft wiederholt
die passionierte Pizzapracht.

Runder Geburtstag

Ein halbes Jahrhundert schon vergangen
und die Schönheit eingefangen
Immer wieder auf's Neue verziert
und wunderbares produziert

Great that you exist
Great as a humanist

Deine Umgebung mit Liebe umhüllt
Und die Seelen ausgefüllt
Mit guten und warmen Gedanken
Immer wieder aufzutanken

Great that you exist
Great as an optimist

Du hast ein riesen Herz und Mitgefühl
Bist eine Zufluchtsinsel im Gewühl
Positiv und voller Tatendrang
Verzauberst du mit deinem Seelenklang

Great that you exist
Great as an actionist

Aufgeschlossen und aufmerksam
Stets wohlwollend und wachsam
Bist du für jeden immer zur Stelle
und schwimmst auf der Daseinswelle

Great that you exist
Great as a reformist

Hast eurer Lieben einen Namen gegeben
und geschaffen ein wundersames neues Leben
Bist eine fantastische Mutter und Lebensbegleiter
Für neue Ideenwelten ein super Wegbereiter

Great that you exist
Great as an idealist

Eine Freundin mit Tiefe und viel Humor
Für viele ein genialer Inspirator
Ein bemerkenswertes Individuum
im Raum-Zeit-Kontinuum

Great that you exist
Great as a philanthropist

Du weisst das Leben zu genießen
Das Sein sei gepriesen
Schön dass es dich gibt hier auf Erden
Mit dir zusammen im Sein und Werden

Let's work hart and have lots of fun
Embrace the earth and the sun
Be happy and full of glee,
occupied and pleasant free.

Let's be creative and never cease
May our growth always increase
Be open minded and aware

to everybody with solid care.

Thanks of being a part
As the Tegernseer wizard
Enchanting life
while we all strife

Wakeup call

The earth is rich
And full of stunning beauty

The world is amazing
And full of great creativity

The planet is awesome
And full of huge ingenuity

And we humans
What do we do

And we people
Where do we go

The soil is rich
And full of giving energy

The galaxy is amazing
And full of endless purity

The mountain is awesome
And full of enormous clarity

What do we do
Taking care at all

Where do we go
Having brains to see

The ocean is rich
And full of precious vitality

The wind is amazing
And full of timeless agility

The sun is awesome
And full of bright singularity

We know what to do
Humbly embrace life

We know where to go
With joy creating the future

Army dreamer

USA, China or Germany
Great business on behalf of innovation
What an integer company
And all on behalf of a peace mission

New technology can be tested
Building up the economy
Money and time was invested
What an upright autonomy

Nations
Ambitions
Threats
Obliteration

Peace without weapons
Innovations through development
Humanity without cannons
New traces to real self-assessment

Corruption needs to be demolished
From the inside the only way
Democracy as well brightly polished
For altruism the entranceway

We can
We will
We do

Traumwandler

Damaskus ein wundervoller Ort
Reich an historischen Ereignissen
Am Anfang stand das Wort
Das Sein mit tausend Erlebnissen

Auf dem Markt voller Gerüche
Hier und da amüsante Sprüche
Ein Gewirr und reges Treiben
Hier würd ich gerne bleiben

Kommt ein blinder Vogel vorbei
Fliegt über die Stadt hinweg
In diesen Lüften ist er frei
Und macht hier seinen Fitness-check

Getestet warden wieder Waffen
Aus dem Westen eingeflogen
Umgeben von Menschenaffen
Schwingt er auf den Lügenwogen

Er singt, schwingt und bezwingt
hinterläßt sogar ne weisse Feder
und in seinen Ohren klingt
wo anders ist das Leben solider

Die Blindheit hilft ja ungemein
wer will den schon was sehen
außer vielleicht den Sonnenschein
und dem wahren Zeitgeschehen.

Unter ihm der Käfig voller Narren
Mit vielen lockeren Schrauben
Da könnt man fast zu Stein erstarren
Bei so nem kranken Glauben

Zum Vögeln kommt er kaum
Wenige sind geblieben
Die meisten längst abgehaun
Und nichts mehr zum Verlieben

We will not cease

Religion is not the reason
To kill and destroy

We will not cease to help
Your terror we detest

We will not cease to create
Your terror we regret

We will not cease to support
Your terror we condemn

We will not cease to construct
Your terror we decry

We will not cease to build up
Your terror we despise

We will not cease to design
Your terror we scrap

We transform the world into a better place
Your terror will disappear

We change the world into a beautiful place
Your terror will vanish

We shape the world into a valuable place
Your terror will pop off

We alter the world into a pleasant place
Your terror will peter out

Our faith can move mountains
Toward love, understanding and altruism

Rege Anteilnahme in Gottesnamen

Mojeju auf dem Sterbebett
Sein Leben war komplett
Viel getan und positives hinterlassen
Mit viel Humor und ganz gelassen

An einen Weltgeist geglaubt
Und alle Religionen erlaubt
Jetzt plötzlich sieht er nur noch weiss
Denkt sich na ja ich bin auch ein Greis

Und wie er so ins Licht geht
Und ihn die ruhige Prise umweht
Begegnet ihm eine warmherzige Gestalt
Und er macht gleich halt

Und fragt wie immer mit Neugier
"wer seid den ihr"
Die Gestalt nicht Frau noch Mann
Zieht Mojeju in seinen Bann
Mit Ungeduld ganz flott
"seid ihr Allah oder Gott"
das Wesen schaut ihn an und lacht
"ich bin die Universumsmacht
und Namen sind nur Schall und Rauch
Manitu das ginge ja auch

Egal wie ihr mich nennt
Und als was ihr mich erkennt
Ich bin nu rein Teil des Ganzen
Und will nur Liebe pflanzen

Doch der Mensch so kleinkariert
Und manchmal fast borniert
Hat ne eindimensioale Sicht
Und versteht die Message nicht

Wir sind alle nu rein Teil
Ist ja schon geil
Wie ihr die Welt so seht
Und mit Ideen verseht

Jeder hat so seine Mission
Und spielt den Universumston
Klar bin ich schlau
Doch weiss ich's nicht genau

Zu welcher Zeit ich handle
Und das IST verwandle
Mojeju hat die Worte vernommen
Und ist nun ganz benommen
"also geht es um Barmerzigkeit
Toleranz und Menschlichkeit"
"Terror ist gegen das Leben
und ein irrsinniges Streben

Egal an was man glaubt
Alles ist im Universum erlaubt
Menschenwürde ist unantastbar
Das ist ja wohl klar

Ein Gott der Krieg will
Ist ein verwerflicher Stil

Die Vielfalt der Kulturen
Hinterläßt die richtigen Spuren

Mojeju versteht nun mehr
Und versinkt im Todesmeer

Equality

Black by nature
Proud by choice
we are all a mixture
and got a voice
to say we are human
and love life
as woman or man
we all strife
to support society
in the best way
we value property
anywhere and anyway
there is no difference
between you and me
listen to our audience
with an open mind to see
regardless the color
it is of no importance
a custom tailor
with brilliance
White by nature
Proud by choice
we are all a mixture
and got a voice.

Uranium

All elements got there attributes
And may contribute
To life itself

Some just at the first sight
May be great and bright
And change

In the beginning the trace
Was the right place
But no more

The waste they produced
And how they were used
Altered utterly

Destruction they involved
And nothing they solved
What a pity

Unfortunately a habit to break
For mankind's sake
Is not easy

Transformations are not easy to do
Neither for me nor for you
Still a need

A new way need to be pursued
Inevitable to distribute

Just wake up

The earth our main resource
Asks for another source
Now to launch

Leave old things behind
And develop your mind
A good idea

Let's start to contemplate
Our own interesting state
Good bye

Der Mann aus Ecuaror

Am Äquator liegt seine Heimat
Die er verlassen hat
Um hier in Deutschland
Seinem neuen Heimatland
Zu schalten
Und zu walten

Er liebt sein Land sehr
Weit entfernt über dem Meer
Wo noch Indigos leben
Und nach Einfachheit streben
Wo Chia und Quinoa ihre Speisen
Gesundheit verheißen
Wo die wilde Natur
unterstützt die Wunderkur

Bayern hat ihn aufgenommen
Hier erhält er sein Einkommen
Und kann davon gut Leben
Und nach Frohsin streben

Wer weiß ob her wieder heim geht
Und dort nach Verbesserung strebt
Wir wollen es ja hoffen
Dass er heiter und offen
Gutes über den Ozean sendet
Und dort das Blatt wendet

Freude möge mit ihm sein
Zu jeder Phase im Sein

Denn wir sind ja eine Welt
Die Toleranz zusammenhält

Die Schönheit existiert überall
Und jeder hat ne Wahl
Sie zu verteilen üverallhin
Darin liegt wohl der Sinn.

Willkommen hier
Das sagen wir
Und verstehen die Leute
Im hier und im heute...

History repeat itself

History repeat itself
Away with all this pelf
The trumpets call
Through the assembly hall
They talk about discrimination
And victimization
The Germans know about it
And found its exit
With the help of the Allies
Where the release lies
And now we face the same
In this sardonic game
A man full of hate
Changing the fate
To another destiny
To reveal and see
Hello again knock knock knock
Ring the alarm clock
We face it again
A disastrous rain
Poking inhumanity
Towards insanity
Misfortune the breeding ground
Wake up and be sound
Come on and be an knight
Honest and bright
Again rose
The white rose
To fight against a man
Just totally inhuman

Understanding

I said a word to express
How to find success
But the other person heard something
And here was the misunderstanding

My language I need to translate
To find the right gate
To the mind of my counterpart
To find another start

May the heart talk to each other
And never ever bother
About stupid negative thought
For which we should not fought

....

HA HA Sarkasmus

Ich sitze hier in aller Stille
Mein Haupt ergraut von der Zeit
Mal ein Trank und Mal ne Pille
Mein Ich schon längst Vergangenheit
Einen Slam für die Masse
Philosophie für ein paar
Ich erhebe meine Ingwertasse
Und preise mein Lebensjahr

White or black

Sorry of being white
Of being bright
My color is like that
And I will not regret
To be what I am
And what I can
I love life
I will strife
I am a world member
And will remember
What lif is all about
Not to shout
But to love and live
To take and give
To work hard
And embrace every start

Donald trumpets

The instrument sounds acute
A bit German before the second war
Often the audience getting rude
Dazzled by the money glamor

The middle class slides in poverty
And the imbalance increasing day by day
What is the price of our liberty
And what amount of wealth we have to pay

Maybe we have to bring into question
Our capitalistic system and change it again
Some pioneers got already a vision
And huge and positive acceptance they obtain

Attention please attention
Watch out where the trumpets call
Hate and brutal aggression
Might cause a national downfall

Humanity needs a good teacher
And a popular preacher

America, America
You were a star

Where is your sparkling light
Suddenly it is gloomy night

Hacking

Should we call them crackers.
those people see themselves as hackers

They wear hats of different colors
Some aim to make money and dollars

A white hat breaks security
for non-malicious integrity

A black hat violates the computer
A special system polluter

A grey hat finds the defect
which one should protect

Tracking
Hacking
Checking

The new pathfinder

The public Interpol

Either D. Ganser or Wikileaks
Truth always speaks
it finds a way to discover
and quickly uncover
what others want to hide
of course worldwide
with a skeleton in their closet
rattling like a skinny rat
in the hand a bloody flower
being just a follower

The main target of a crook
to enrich one's checkbook
Or power to get and gain
Singing in the control-rain

Die Brille

Ich stehe auf
und setz sie auf
ups da ist ein Fleck
den mach ich weg

Wow ich sehe was
durchs geschliffene Glas
Mensch klasse Errungenschaft
die Weitblick schafft

Früher gab es viel Kummer
Heute ist's ne geile Nummer,
die Schwäche aufzuheben
und ihr Schärfe zu geben.

Heut bin ich der Student
mit Nickelbrille und nem Hemd
Morgen der coole Gestalter
mit Ray Ban und als Unterhalter

Den Blick auf die Welt
so wie sie mir gefällt
und wenn ich keinen Bock hab
nehm ich sie einfach ab.

Special glasses to see

Everywhere I see pulchritude
Kids just happy and cute
Flowers blooming bright
Moonshine in the night
Here and there a kiss
with warm happiness.
The boisterously wind
upraising the mind.
Throughout the years
music in the ears.
One my way an old apple tree
with his fruits amazing to see.
Upon the mountain peak
silence to seek.
Manmade sculpture across the street
Awesome impressions to meet
Gardens with a fantastic view
There a spreading yew.
Sometimes a small waterfall
illuminates at nightfall.
A delicacy for the senses
full of tasty conveniences.
Technological elegancy
exceptional and fancy
The glasses to wear I decide
Universal wide

Almond Shaming

They are delicious
Thanks nature for this fruit
We are almost voracious
And enjoy them intuit

We make Marzipan
With honey for the winter time
In a cake-pan
Yum yum very tasty

Your creator a beautiful tree
widely ramified
awesome and gluten-free
seriously great

You need lots of water to grow
Nothing unusual to say
For this gift you virtually bestow
So why blaming you

Normally you find the right place
Where you want to be raised
But as you know the human race
Show you where to stay

Toilettengang

Das Wasser drängt
und steht schon an
wird dicht gedrängt
vom großen Mann

Mit schnellen Schritten
wird der Raum gesucht
schon weit fortgeschritten
hier naht die Zuflucht

Endlich alles loslassen
Was für ne Wasserflut
Ne große Wurst hinterlassen
Ah wie gut das tut

Puh auf die letzte Sekunde
Grad noch geschafft
Meine eigne Biostunde
Mit Zuckersaft

Feldenkrais

Awareness Through Movement
A certain way to understand
Body and Mature Behavior
From the ex- to the interior

New patterns of repeated motions
Slow and gentle actions
To impart new habits
In the physical orbits

By expanding the self-image
And exchange personal baggage
through movement sequences
gain new life experiences.

The self that are out of awareness
Bringing to a novel success
With all the greatness
To boldness

Ellbogen - Gesellschaft

Ich bin besser
Ich weiß mehr
Ich bin kesser
Ich lieb's sehr

Was willst du mit Werten
Die kann man nicht verwerten
Nehmen und raffen
Was gibt's da zu gaffen

Ich bin klasse
Ich kann viel
Ich hab Rasse
Ich hab ein Ziel

Was willst du mit Sozialen
Kannst ne Illusion dir malen
Kämpfen und schlagen
Der Macht nachjagen

Ich bin spitze
Ich bin schnell
Ich habe Hitze
Ich bin materiell

Was willst du mit Achtsamkeit
Verrenn dich in die Menschlichkeit
Du hast es einfach nicht erkannt
Und wirst halt überrannt

Du Weichei, nichts in der Hose
Ich schenk dir ne Trauerrose

Geburt

So eine Geburt
Hat es in sich
Zuerst kommen die Wehen
Ganz plötzlich unbesehen
Die Blüte bricht auf
Und schon geht es los
Der Papa hält die Hand
Und verliert seinen Verstand
Die Mama presst und drückt
Und vom jetzt und hier entrückt
Die Abstände werden kürzer
Das Pressen wird stärker
Juhu der Kopf schaut raus
Welch süße kleine Maus
Hier die Arme und Beine
Da ist sie die Kleine
Wunderbar ein neues Leben
Der Papa ganz begeistert
Er darf sie als erster halten
Zuerst noch ganz verhalten
dann strahlt er über beide Ohren
Er ist Vater geworden
Ganz sachte legt er sie
Der Mama in den Arm
Wie erklären was man hier spürt
Das Elternglück hat die Seele berührt
Genial und wundervoll
Klasse und einfach toll

The Prince

Only the expenditure of one's own resources is harmful
Therefore be always with your decisions foresightful
Nothing feeds upon itself as liberality does in general
Therefore be mainly target-oriented and liberal
The question is whether it is better to be loved than feared
Of course the best would be, to be in both an expert
People are generally self-interested,
Especially when they are battle-tested
They admire honor, generosity and courage
But these virtues are not their natural entourage
Power need to be maintained in a certain way
And which direction to take in our modern day

Sanftmut

Bei Herrschern galt sie als Tugend
Noch nicht so ausgeprägt in der Jugend
Sie ist eine Art Behutsamkeit
Eine Milde und Zahmheit

Als Kardinalstugend der Menschlichkeit
Angesiedelt im Bereich der Tapferkeit
Die Sanftmütigen sind glückselig
Aufmerksam und sehr feinfühlig

Ohne Zorn und Rachsucht
In der Hand die Liebesfrucht
ein angenehmes und geduldiges Verhalten
und in Freundlichkeit schalten und walten

Sanftmütig und rein
Edelmütig und fein
Ein wunderbarer Charakterzug
Ein ehrenwerter Seelenflug

Expansion

Positive Einschätzungen der Wirtschaftssubjekte,
günstige Produktionsbedingungen und Aufschwung
das sind der Wirtschaft wichtige Objekte
und für den Freihandel eine wesentliche Bedingung.
Die stete Zunahme der Entfernung
weit voneinander entfernter Objekte im Raum
gemäß dem Urknall die Erklärung
als Ausdehnung in unserem Spielraum
Kolonialismus eine weitere Möglichkeit
mehr Länder wurden erobert über die Zeit
ganz gleich es ist alles eine Expansion
und eine unvorstellbare Dimension

IQ Test

Was für ein sinnvoller Test
Er sagt alles über den Menschen aus
Und gibt ihm noch den Rest
Verkriech dich lieber in dein Schneckenhaus

Emotionale Intelligenz wird hier nicht gemessen
Oder Kreativität im Allgemeinen
Sind ja auch keine wirtschaftlichen Interessen
Die muss man hier verneinen

Was so manches Genie wohl in sich trug
Wäre mal interessant
Ein kleiner Mozart auf Instrumentenflug
Geistvoll und brillant

So ist es mit der Intelligenz
Und der Kompetenz
Testen kann man viel
Im IQ-Rätselspiel

Schweißgeruch

Neben mir ist ein Gestank
Ich kann ihn schon nicht mehr riechen
Ich wird hier langsam krank
Am liebsten möchte ich mich verkriechen

Eine Folterform der besonderen Art
Subtil geht es in Mark und Bein
Warum bleibt es mir nicht erspart
Das kann doch gar nicht sein

Ein Horrortrip dieser Schweißgeruch
Ein Grauen sonders gleichen
Und jeder kleine Fluchtversuch
Steht im negativen Zeichen

Digital Darkness

All of a sudden no more electricity
Going back to simplicity
The past disappears within a second
The advice fails to respond

Terrible what to do with the time
Not captured by the screen
For the life a new colorful prime
A silky changing sheen

What a progress
Moving happiness
Within digital darkness
A great success

Hooligans

Pures Testosteron
Kommt zur Explosion
Aufgestauter Hass
Ist das Pulverfass
Besonders beim Fußball
Kommt es zum Knall
Und die lodernde Glut
die reine Zerstörungswut
kann sich entladen
auf den Fan-Barrikaden
Verluste gibt es immer
Hier und da Gewimmer
So ist es bei Randalen
Dazu gehören Qualen
Prügeln ohne Sinn
Ein magerer Gewinn.

Der Nörgler

Seine Grundhaltung ist der Pessimismus
Ständig hat er was zu beklagen
Und muss was Negatives sagen
Da ist kaum Platz für Positivismus

Energieräuber kann man sie auch nennen
Sie ziehen dich in den Abgrund rein
Und oft nach kurzer Zeit wird man erkennen
Wie grauenvoll der Sonnenschein

Letztlich wird der Meckerer einsam
Und fällt noch mehr in eine Depression
Für andere ist es leider ratsam
Ihn allein zu lassen in seiner Aggression

Mähh mähh nur weiter so
Arme Ziege hier der Flo

News

What kind of news we watch day by day
Most of time just negative stories

What does these news create within us
Most of time just negative emotion

What should we do with all those negations
Most time just change the channel

What is the responsibility of the press
Most time just to talk about truth

What kind of truth is out there in the world
Most time just fascinating stories

What do these stories create within us
Most of the time just happiness

What should we do with this positivity
Most of the time just spread it

Stranded in Germany

Mom and Dad said escape
find another landscape
You are young and strong
sing the freedom song
We fled from Syria
And arrived in Bavaria
First we stayed in shanties
and had no guaranties
But the folks wanted to support
and opened up a new port
Beside a home and provisions
The first we got was education
Soon we felt glad and secure
within this Bavarian culture
With their altruism and assistance
we gained self-reliance
In our homeland it is still drear,
may peace soon appear
And we can give back this openness
the people here express

Galgenzähler

Der Galgenzähler misst den Geigenhumor
Nach dem Verhalten zu urteilen sehr verhalten.
Mit Gewalten verwalten oder schalten
Total egal ob Trübsal oder Qual

Das Lachen bleibt als Poesie der Ironie
Und wir versehen das Vergehen mit Vergeben
Denn wir sehen in dem Leben ein Vergehen
Ein Mist wie's ist so ist's

Warten

Auf was warten wir oft
Und es kommt ganz unverhofft
Auf was wir gewartet haben
Konnten wir uns nicht laben
So warten wir aus das Eine
Und was anderes zappelt an der Fangleine
Das Warten hatte sich gelohnt
Und wurde gut belohnt
So ist es mit der Zeit
Und ihrer Einsatzmöglichkeit

Da wartet man auf Godot und wartet vor sich hin
Na da sag ich mal das macht ja richtig Sinn

Die neuen PolitikerInnen

Klar gehöre ich einer Partei an
Und dann und wann
Kommuniziere ich meine eigenen Ansichten
Und werde meine Partei auch richten

Es geht mir um das Volk und unsere Werte
Und jeder ist in irgendetwas Experte
Dann frag ich den und höre zu
Denn Gemeinschaftlich geht alles im Nu

Konformität nur wenn es unbedingt sein muss
Wir haben Demokratie und kein Kommunismus
Eine Vielfalt von Ideen und Vokabularien
Ein Verändern mit Zukunft Szenarien

Also egal ob Demokrat oder Republikaner
Ob Deutscher oder Amerikaner
Unser Ziel ist soziale Gerechtigkeit
Und daran fehlt es noch weit

Raise our flags

Why there is no flag
Swinging in the air
To say we share
And fight back

Wherever a bomb may explode
Iran, Irak or France, no matter where
It's a terrible episode
And it's us all who care

Ministers and presidents
You are the nation hands
You have to raise our condolence
To every country for nonviolence

Let's hoist the flag to half-mast
And be the idealistic phantast
Who believes in peace
Which may increase

Flame and game

I just saw the EM soccer game
Full of emotion and inner flame
And asked myself what it might be
That we are special and full of glee

And I realized that is our passion
And everybody's own vision
Like Ronaldo full of obedience obligation
Finding the right soccer navigation

The ballad of insanity

Some people kill the thing they love
Some others the thing they hate

Some people kill with their weapons
Some others with a flattering word

Some people kill out of kneejerk reaction
Some others brutally calculating

Some people kill with a great speech
Some others without a tone

Some people kill with great joy
Some others with a tear

Mankind seems to be a killing field
With dead bodies and souls

It is a contradiction to men's intellect
It is a contradiction to the beauty of us all

We want to help each other
we want to serve with glee

Destruction sail your way
Creativity will stay

What makes us special

I just saw the EM soccer game
Full of emotion and fame
And asked myself what it might be
That we are speccial and full gf glee

And I realized that is is our passion
And everybodys own vision
Like Ronaldo full of obediance obligation
Finding the real mission

I am a cosmopolitan

How to encounter terrible destruction and insane killing?
maybe just with love and positive thoughts!?

I sing I sing The Ballad of Reading Gaol
And see the killing of a soul

I am I am an Arab with a great heart
And of this world a part

I am I am a Jewish with great tolerance
In this world I love to dance

I am I am a Christian with joy and happiness
In this world a great success

I am I am a Buddhist with love and peace
In this world it might increase

I am I am a Hindu with great believe
In this world to achieve

I am I am an Atheist with huge respect
In this world to expect

I am I am a Shintoist with attentiveness to all
In this world to install

I am I am thousand things like you as well
We all want create heaven instead of hell

We are We are full of strength and full of dignity
I this world exchange humanity

I sing I sing the ballade of the understanding zone
In this world with a charming tone

Renewable Energy

What's the hitch?
The earth is rich

We take with caution
And right proportion

Batteries will get more efficient
And almost self-sufficient

Wind or water are everywhere
And energy is in the air

The Croatian guy knew a lot
And J. P. Morgan was in the plot

Important things just disappeared
Yes, yes that's weird

But what was salt for a special day
Was money the new beauty clay

As humans are not stupid at all
They are clever and will install

An energy that lasts for a long time
Sure of course there will be crime

Without rascals and crooks
We will write just boring books

So time goes on and human sex
Will be sustainable and relax

Aleppo

Destruction
Killing fields
....
....
....
....
Insane
No brain

Born As A White Feeling As A Black

I was born as a white
Beautiful and bright
But I feel like a black
prejudices to reflected
We are humans with love inside
Full of understanding and pride

No words to be told
Humanity we al hold
In our hand with humble
Sometimes we stumble
And still we love life
And strife
To peace and happiness
And own fulfilled success

By nature I am white
By choice I am black
Nothing to regret
It is right

Music Reflect Time (Thanks To Michael Jackson)

We are the one who decide
We are the one who change
We can be full of pride
We can be full of exchange

We are Musk, Einstein or like all other geniuses
We are the ones who create a better civilization
We can generate a world of million positive uses
We can create an universe of cross-fertilization

We are humans with love inside
We can be a species of perfection

Whatever we can
And whatever we are
We design our way
And for what we pray

Whatever we are
And whatever we can
We are the creators
And the worthy investors

Ridiculous Hope - No

I always hoped that the humans change
I always hoped that the humans understand
I always hoped that the humans love

I still do even so I see all the million killings
I still do even so I see all the million hatreds
I still do even so I see all the million misleading's

What is the balm for the soul
What is important to everybody
What is the treasure in our life

Every single person aims to love
Every single person aims to transfer knowledge
Every single person aims to be good

Some are looking for power
Some are looking for wealth
Some are looking for fame

We all let them find there way of universal success
We all let them find there way to love themselves
We all let them find there way to be happy

Sooner or later all borders will disappear
Sooner or later life's symphony is heard
Sooner or later humanity will win

Diamonds, Just Diamonds

Diamonds everywhere, sparkling in the sunshine
Beautiful and awesome for the eyes
And even the snow in the air is like million stars

It is cold outside, but the heat of this spectacle
Keeps us warm and full of glee

The mountains are dressed all in white
Like the brides of the winter time

Here and there are icicles hanging down
Like ear rings to decorate nature

The music of the air is muffled and soft
Keeps us in the land of fairytales

Glitter everywhere, lightening the psyche
Indescribable wonderful for the heart
Like a wedding of the season with the earth

Hollywood Speaks Out

Free press
Free express
Free speech
To reach

The Artist aim
Is to proclaim
The reality
and integrity

The Oscar a tribute
An honorable repute
To understand characters
And feel them as actors

Like poets or musicians
Wizards and magicians
They reflect on stage
The current age

And even better
Time does not matter
Beyond all bounds
They reveal backgrounds

As a book of pictures
Arrivals and departures
Of human ambitions
With great emotions

This is the target and goal
To show the beautiful soul
Of our human nature
As a vulnerable creature

Multicultural with pride
Strong and bright
Pictures of the la la land
Powerful and confidant

Always The Same

Who ever it is
I will treat him like a king
I will treat her like a queen
No matter what they did or we
Still attentiveness will be
A part of my courtesy
With love and universal harmony
Politeness to every creature in this universe
An inner humanity to rehearse
Respect a perfect match
All the time to catch
So let us be the masters of our aim
Innocent thought so proclaim.

I Am The President

I am the President
and humble toward this task

I am the President
and know about this responsibility

I am the President
and have great dream of tolerance

I am the President
and support open diplomacy

I am the President
and review myself as a world citizen

I am the President
and believe in sustainability

I am the President
and understand all my countrymen

I am the President
and facilitate education for everybody

I am the President
and assist all human people

I am President
and encourage peace and understanding

I am the President
and will fight with words and without weapons

I am the President
and will fight against climatic change

I am the President
and will fight for a better world

Humble and integer
Peaceful and liberal

Intercultural and international
with our culture in mind

America, America

I am American and believe in freedom
I am American and believe in equality
I am American and believe in humanity
I am American and believe in love

No matter what religions we have
No matter what background we have
No matter what physical statement we have
No matter what mental statement we have

We are beyond people of hatred
We are beyond narrow minded creatures
We are beyond social discrimination
We are beyond negative statements

Yes we can change into good
Yes we can open new borders
Yes we can support education
Yes we can create a beautiful state

Review And Change Your Country

Where they come from?
Why they want to enter our countries?
Some flee from war
Some others from corruption
Some do not want to starve
Some others escape dictatorship

What can they do?
When is time to fight?
They have to change their society
They have to go for freedom
They have to invest in education
They have to create beauty

And we, you and me
And we the countries of democracy
We just can seed an open mind
We just can give knowledge
We just can be an advisor
We just can support harmony

And those who fled and found a country
Should go back to help their countrymen
Healing comes from inside
Healing hands we give

Heal yourself and create a better world

Humaneness

Invest invest invest
in weapons I suggest

Ouch ridiculous I would say
we finally have to repay

The inner sun a central aim
where humanity we proclaim

Amazing that Pavlov is still there
where destruction People prepare

Doing what them were told
Ascending the brainwashed scaffold

Hey there friends
we got it in our Hands

Let fear never conquer our mind
For the benefit of mankind

We are the force
to endorse
a species of gloriousness
and grandness

We all have to be upright
sensitive and bright
and embrace life with glee
with a beautiful future to foresee

2 Go 4 It

I was full of fear
but switched the gear
and rose my hat
and fought instead

Love I wanted to find
but I was blind
not wanting to be hurt
with a fast spurt

Love might also kill
and be a bitter pill
but to run away
not the perfect sway

I was full of fear
but switched the gear
and rose my hat
and fought instead

To act brave and responsible
often hardly comprehensible
one has to be honorable and bold
Murphy's law is seriously quiet old

To be a bastion of calm
to find the adequate balm
often just pain
again and again.

I was full of fear
but switched the gear
and rose my hat
and fought instead

To stand up for your ideas
cry and laugh tears
be open for up and downs
feeling the inner clowns

Taking all challenges with glee
plant the courtesy tree
sometimes we have to fight
like an exceptional knight

I was full of fear
but switched the gear
and rose my hat
and fought instead

Moving Mountains

I wonder how man just acts
Because of angst and fear
Reflecting not the true facts
And make them unclear

I wonder how man just plays
A game of blames and claims
And incredible unworthy prays
For his own little fame

I wonder how long it will take
That man go for just the good
And realizes that selfishness is fake
And needs to be universal understood

I wonder how long the eyes are blind
Unable to see the beauty to share
And what huge richness we can be find
By watching each other with care

The wonder will come
with smooth steps to everyone

The wonder is near
with more and more old souls

Wonders are like that
suddenly they exist

Index

EPILOG

Es fing an
mit dem Anstieg
immer höher und höher,
das Leben war gut zu einem.
Aktionen verfolgten immer ihr Ziel
und erreichten es mit einer Leichtigkeit.
A gmade Wiesen wie man so schön sagt.
Kein Widerstand, alles flutschte wie es sollte
Das nenne ich mal Glück auf allen Ebenen im Sein!
Wie das Leben so ist gibt es ja andere Zeiten
Da kommen dann die Steine des Weges,
und man darf sie von dannen tragen.
Egal das gehört auch zum Sein!
Auf und nieder immer wieder,
besingen wir das Leben.
Amüsantes Streben
Und hört nicht auf

Zeitfracht Medien GmbH
Ferdinand-Jühlke-Straße 7
99095 Erfurt, Deutschland
produktsicherheit@kolibri360.de